THE
PEOPLE MANAGER'S
POCKETBOOK

By Ian Fleming

Drawings by Phil Hailstone

D0657830

"Packed with concise information and suggestions. The message is never lost."
Duncan Monroe, Business Planning Executive, Dalgety Food Ingredients

"This excellent handbook provides particularly useful advice for those difficult personal
situations which often arise at work."

Michael Lockha Shrewsbury Health Library **Games Federation**

CONTENTS

MANAGING: WHAT'S DIFFERENT? 1
New and not enjoying it, staff know more than you, people resisting change

DEALING WITH PEOPLE 13
No support from boss, motivation drops, a poor performer, difficult individual, persistent latecomer, boss decides without you, opposing views on staff, clash over appraisal, heavy drinker, person has B.O.

DEVELOPING ABILITIES 53
Difficulty settling in, reluctance to go on courses, business 1st – people 2nd, a slow learner, appraisals not working

BUILDING TEAMS 75
People not interested, leadership style resented, individual is isolated, leadership challenged

ACHIEVING RESULTS 93
Plans always go wrong, staff produce work late, uneven workload

USEFUL READING 106

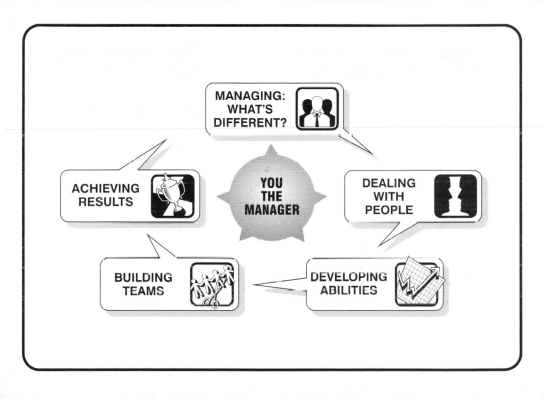

INTRODUCTION

This book is intended for people who find themselves in charge of others. Although technically qualified, you may lack the people skills needed to be effective.

The People Manager's Pocketbook aims to fill the gap by offering pointers to those tricky situations for which nobody is prepared. Each example is split into three parts:

Signs	- that indicate there's a problem
Possible reasons	- as to why it could be happening
Practical suggestions	- a range of ideas to follow

For the sake of clarity, we have alternated between male and female throughout the examples, rather than using the cumbersome ploy of he/she.

Points to bear in mind
When faced with difficult situations:

- Don't panic; think before you act
- Be clear of the facts; don't act on emotion
- If there are procedures in your organisation, follow them
- Keep a note of what you do; you may need it later
- Don't be afraid to ask for help, either when the situation arises or, afterwards, to talk through what happened

MANAGING:
WHAT'S DIFFERENT

WHAT'S INVOLVED

Moving into a managerial role involves making changes from the way you previously performed.

FROM		TO
'Doing' the job	➡	an uncertain 'supervisory' role
Using technical skills	➡	placing emphasis on people and admin skills
Using well-developed skills	➡	learning new ones
Tasks being delegated to you	➡	having to delegate to others
Controlling the output	➡	being judged on the output and quality of others
Having knowledge	➡	managing others, often with more knowledge

- Often people
    - fail to recognise and understand these differences
    - are not helped to develop the necessary skills
    - as a result, neither perform nor enjoy the job.

NEW & NOT ENJOYING IT?

SIGNS

You find yourself:

- Working long hours, taking work home (family complaints?)
- Finding it difficult to supervise people who are friends and ex-colleagues
- In a job that holds little satisfaction
- Showing signs of stress
  - physical (tiredness, headaches)
  - emotional (irritability, tension)
  - mental (worry, poor decisions)
- Believing that life will be easier once you've mastered the job
- Not being able to talk to anyone - it must be you, everyone else appears to be coping
- Being put to the test by staff (eg: they stand around chatting) – how do you handle it?

(3)

NEW & NOT ENJOYING IT?

POSSIBLE REASONS

- Perhaps you are struggling to make the changes needed to do the job.
  You could be passing through the stages of:

Shock	- the job is not as you expected
Denial	- perhaps it's not as bad as you first thought
Depression	- it really is bad and things can't carry on
Accepting reality	- something has to change
Testing	- trying new ways and seeing reactions
Finding what works	- rejecting some approaches, building on others
Acceptance	- of the changes you've made and a difference in your life

Based on the work of Adams, Hayes, Hopkins: 'Transitions' published by Martin Robertson

NEW & NOT ENJOYING IT?

PRACTICAL SUGGESTIONS

- Acknowledge what's happening (a new role; want to do well; need to keep on good terms with others)
- Ask your boss for help
- Do something to establish yourself
- Concentrate on priorities
- Learn to deal with difficult people (see pages 29-30 for some tips)
- Seek some training; remember there are other (often more effective) ways to develop yourself than going on courses (see page 61)
- Be positive; try to focus on other aspects of the job, eg:
  - you are the person trusted with getting things done
  - you have power and influence over what's happening
  - you possess skills and abilities

'The doors of opportunity are marked push.'

(5)

STAFF KNOW MORE THAN YOU?

SIGNS

You find yourself managing staff with more day to day knowledge of what's happening, or greater technical knowledge and skills.

Typically:

- They use jargon that you don't know
- Give explanations that you don't understand, and, what's more, cannot argue against
- You find yourself by-passed; people in the organisation go direct to them for an answer/explanation
- Feel yourself losing touch
- Try to keep yourself updated but things change so fast
- Have other demands on your time (eg: meetings, dealing with customers); your intentions are good but the situation is hopeless

STAFF KNOW MORE THAN YOU?

POSSIBLE REASONS

- The higher you move up the ladder into 'management' the further you could be getting away from the jobs that people do

SENIOR MANAGEMENT

OPERATOR

PLAN CONTROL

DOING

- As an 'operator' you became an expert at your job
- In a managerial role you often lose that expertise and spend your time doing other things, such as planning and controlling the work of your section
- Sadly, the higher you rise the less of an 'expert' you are likely to become

STAFF KNOW MORE THAN YOU?

PRACTICAL SUGGESTIONS

- Recognise that you're not alone (managing others with more knowledge is becoming commonplace in today's business environment)
- Talk to people on a one-to-one basis:
  - identify what skills you have between you
  - find out how they can help you,
  - explain how you can help them, eg: by promoting their ideas and giving them credit
  - make sure you keep each other involved
- Ask the dumb questions, especially if you're not sure what they are talking about and/or its implications
- Don't get hung up on what you **don't** know
- Seek to educate people; experts can sometimes become rather narrow in their outlook

PEOPLE RESISTING CHANGE?

SIGNS

As a (new) manager you identify areas where changes need to be made. However, your staff react in the following ways:

- They give you a list of reasons why ideas will not work, eg:
  - *'We've always done it this way; it works, so why change it?'*
- There's a shaking of heads - poor/no eye contact
- They quote examples from the past: *'We've tried it before'*
- They gang up with others to resist new ways
- They say 'yes' and do nothing
- They're always too busy to listen to your new ideas
- They set you up to fail!

PEOPLE RESISTING CHANGE?

POSSIBLE REASONS

You
- You're new to the job and want to make an impression
- Seek to change things - possibly unnecessarily
- May not have thought through the implications and how to sell change to others

Them
- Personal dislike/distrust of you
- Fear of the unknown/insecurity/fear of experimenting
- Historical factors, relating to how previous situations have been handled
- Misinformation; don't understand what's happening and why
- People's core skills are threatened
- Low trust within the organisation
- Fear of failure, making mistakes, looking stupid
- Strong peer group norms to conform to
- Change comes from management; therefore, oppose it

PEOPLE RESISTING CHANGE?

PRACTICAL SUGGESTIONS

- As with any change, think it through and plan all stages, eg:
  - Why are you changing? Is it your idea or something that's been imposed?
  - What are you trying to change - a method of working or the direction of your business?
  - What's going for it; what's going against it?
  - Who will be the winners/losers?
  - What could go wrong?
  - How will you overcome any problems?
  - Who do you need to get on your side and by when?
  - Do you know the timescale and the details of what has to be achieved?
  - What support can you get from your boss or colleagues?

Remember, there's no substitute for planning.

PEOPLE RESISTING CHANGE?

PRACTICAL SUGGESTIONS

- Talk to them as individuals about the changes **but** don't be surprised if they behave differently when they are with their peers/in a group

- Involve them:
  - discuss what needs to be done and get their ideas
  - acknowledge any difficulties, but sell the benefits as you see them
  - sow seeds to get them interested
  - listen to any worries and concerns expressed; how can these be overcome?
  - confront any potential problems at an early stage

- If they resist (there's a fair chance that they will):
  - agree a compromise: a trial period using a combination of their ideas and yours
  - don't push it; you may be able to live without the change
  - put it on ice: come back to it when the time/climate is more favourable

DEALING WITH PEOPLE

YOU CAN'T AVOID IT

- Management is about dealing with people, both internally and externally
- Often success depends on getting people to work (willingly) both for and with you; it sounds easy but problems can occur with:
  - the difficult and unpredictable person
  - people you know but who surprise you by their (in)actions
  - having to deal with people you don't necessarily like
  - communication breakdowns: was it your fault or theirs?
- The key to dealing with people is the need to adapt the approach to individuals; what works for one may not necessarily work for another
- Insights as well as an understanding of people and personalities may help you deal with some of the situations that follow

NO SUPPORT FROM BOSS?

SIGNS

On a variety of issues you feel that your boss is letting you down.

- He is:
  - not available when needed
  - critical of your ideas
  - always in a hurry ('make it quick')

- He says:
  'If that's what you want to do, go ahead and I will back you'; but then:
  - doesn't
  - criticises you afterwards
  - holds it against you, often for years to come
- Is friendlier with the staff than with you
- Offers very little feedback; you don't know where you stand
- Gives you rope - what is to stop you hanging yourself?

NO SUPPORT FROM BOSS?

POSSIBLE REASONS

- Boss believes that you are wrong; in his experience:
  - it will not work
  - you haven't thought through all the implications
- Self-protection
- Is 'two-faced' and, deep down, doesn't like you
- Is not skilled at handling staff
- Does not trust your judgement, especially if you have made mistakes in the past
- Has a demanding job and is often pre-occupied when you talk to him; therefore, he may not have grasped the total picture
- Politically, on the issues in question, boss gains very little from supporting you
- There has been a breakdown in communication between you

DEALING WITH PEOPLE

NO SUPPORT FROM BOSS?

PRACTICAL SUGGESTIONS

- Consider your options:
  - to do nothing would be to duck the issue
  - at the very least you have to find out why you are getting no support (you may learn something)
- Think back and ask yourself:
  - Am I sure that my boss doesn't support me? (What are the facts or is it just a hunch?)
  - How important is it? Do I get support on the things that matter?
- What pressures is he under at present?
- Could you present your ideas more successfully? Tips Include:
  - thinking how your boss likes things presented, eg: big picture or details
  - asking what might be in it for him
  - anticipating objections he might raise
  - keeping your presentation simple and businesslike

NO SUPPORT FROM BOSS?

PRACTICAL SUGGESTIONS

Use the 3-part assertion message as a way of confronting your boss:

1. Prepare a non-judgemental description of his behaviour:
   - describe in **specific** rather than vague terms
   - limit yourself to **behavioural** descriptions; don't attempt to draw inferences
   - make it as brief as possible

2. Disclose your feelings:
   - How do you feel about the effects of the other person's behaviour on you?

3. Say how this behaviour affects you

EXAMPLE:

Behaviour description	*'When you disagreed with my decision on ...*
Disclosure of feelings	*I felt annoyed and let down ...*
Effect on you	*because I was counting on your support to make it happen.'*

DEALING WITH PEOPLE

MOTIVATION DROPS?

SIGNS

You have a good member of staff who, for no apparent reason, appears to lose motivation. You might notice:

- Work output falls
- Lack of interest in job/organisation
- Person lets it be known that she is 'looking around for another job'
- Work is delayed; even the simplest job becomes a chore
- Arrives late - but leaves on time
- Clock watches - sighs a lot!
- Her behaviour is rubbing off on others; all of a sudden many people seem disgruntled and unhappy

(19)

MOTIVATION DROPS?

POSSIBLE REASONS

- Motivation is a complex and personal topic:
  - what motivates one person may not motivate another
  - it changes; individuals are motivated by particular things at certain times

- Consider what could be causing the situation; it could be:
  - the job no longer holds any challenge
  - lack of job security
  - money - not getting paid enough for the position and responsibilities
  - status - not being recognised
  - working conditions, which can affect people's abilities to concentrate (eg: open plan offices are often difficult to work in)
  - relationships with others
  - quality of supervision or lack of it
  - too much red tape making life difficult
  - something outside work

MOTIVATION DROPS?

PRACTICAL SUGGESTIONS

- Consider how well you know the person:
  - Has it happened before?
  - When did you last talk to her about work or hobbies?
- Be clear about what you want the person to do differently/better in the future
- Remember that everybody (however lazy) is motivated to do **something**; the problem is that they are not motivated to do what **you** want them to do
- Tell the individual what she is doing and the effect it's having. This involves giving feedback on:
  - the behaviour **not** the individual
  - what you have seen happening **not** what you've inferred
  - sharing ideas, **not** giving advice
  - exploring alternatives, **not** providing answers

MOTIVATION DROPS?

PRACTICAL SUGGESTIONS

- Don't forget that motivation is a two-way process: there are certain things you can do; the rest is down to the individual (you can take a horse to water but you can't make it drink)

- Consider what the person is good at and what she enjoys doing, then look at the job; what chance is there for these skills and abilities to be used? Could you build in more opportunities?

- Build a challenge into the job:
  - can you give her something that she hasn't done before yet is well within her scope
  - can you let her set her own objectives (see page 98 for details on objective setting)

- Offer help in the form of counselling if the problem is of a personal nature

A POOR PERFORMER?

SIGNS

You find yourself managing an individual whose work can only be described as 'poor'. Typically:

- The person never achieves - poor performance becomes the norm and consequently standards drop
- He cannot be relied on to deliver - misses deadlines
- Mistakes are made - he blames others and resents being spoken to
- You find yourself spending a lot of time with him
- When put under pressure the person panics
- It's having a knock-on effect:
  - morale drops
  - people start to complain
  - others are having to pick up additional work which leads to resentment/bad atmosphere

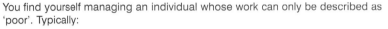

If the poor performer is managing/supervising others, the difficulties are compounded!

(23)

DEALING WITH PEOPLE

A POOR PERFORMER?
POSSIBLE REASONS

- He has reached the limit of capability
- Is not aware that performance is poor
- Has never been confronted/told before
- It could be:
  - **you**: eg: standards are too high for the individual
  - **the work**: eg: too difficult, too much, person becomes demotivated
  - **the individual**: eg: unhappy, in poor health, lazy
- Apathy amongst management; people are aware of the situation but nobody is prepared to do anything about it

A POOR PERFORMER?

PRACTICAL SUGGESTIONS

- Get to the core of the problem, don't simply address the symptoms
- Remember that:
  - as a manager you are responsible for the performance of your staff
  - your credibility could be on the line if you don't do anything about it (irrespective of what's happened in the past)
  - covering up for the individual will be evading the issue
  - if someone claims to have a certain skill they must be able to demonstrate it
  - you can dismiss someone for poor performance if they are:
  - ▲ incapable of performing
  - ▲ capable, but their work falls below the required standard

Ask yourself if the person falls into either of these categories; if 'yes', start to put in place any company procedures for dealing with these situations

A POOR PERFORMER?

PRACTICAL SUGGESTIONS

- Go back to basics, eg:
  - What do you expect the person to do?
  - How well/ to what standard should he perform?

- Identify where he may be falling down; be specific and try to establish why this is.

- Obtain agreement on:
  - what needs to be done
  - what help is needed
  - a timescale

- Put the points in writing (this is essential, especially if your plan fails to bring about an improvement in performance)

- Give any support that you agreed to provide

- Monitor the person's performance, and take any action that may be necessary as you go along

'DIFFICULT' INDIVIDUAL?

SIGNS

Have you come across an individual who performs well but whose behaviour can only be described as 'difficult'? Someone who:

- Disagrees a lot
- Is unco-operative
- Often avoids eye contact
- Is unpredictable (blows hot and cold) or moody
- Gets angry/annoyed with you and others
- Sometimes acts the 'loner' (may not mix with the rest of the group/team)
- Says 'yes' and does nothing
- Does the minimum required and little more
- Behaves badly to other people, eg:
  - attempts to put people down (in front of others)
  - makes sexist/racist remarks
  - goes behind people's backs

'DIFFICULT' INDIVIDUAL?

POSSIBLE REASONS

- Holds a grudge
- Lonely or shy
- Troubled by something outside work
- Dislikes the job
- Resents you or your seniority
- Dislikes being supervised
- Feels badly done by
- Frustrated
- Feels anxious and nervous, which can affect behaviour
- May face conflict over values, beliefs or personality
- Could be working on the wrong/ different assumptions
- Is playing a game

'DIFFICULT' INDIVIDUAL?

PRACTICAL SUGGESTIONS

- Accept that it may not be the person who is difficult, but her behaviour
- Think about the 'difficult' person:
  - In what situation is she difficult?
  - What is it about her behaviour that's difficult?
  - What triggers that behaviour in the first place?
  - How do you react when she behaves in that way?
  - Is there a pattern emerging?
- Identify the behaviour that you find difficult: can you put a label on it? (If so this will help you deal with it)
- Recognise how you feel when it happens, eg: overwhelmed/helpless; not in control; aggressive/worked up
- Demonstrate that you are in control; avoid showing anger or frustration

29

'DIFFICULT' INDIVIDUAL?

PRACTICAL SUGGESTIONS

- Consider your options, eg:
    - do nothing, especially if you suspect that you know the underlying reason for the behaviour
    - learn to live with it
    - stand up to her
    - go for a compromise
    - play for time
    - behave in the same way towards the person
    - use the power of your position to put her down
    - ask for help to be able to deal with her

- Develop your skills to deal with people/situations, eg: become more assertive which will help you:
    - control your emotions
    - tell people how you are feeling, the effect of their behaviour and what you want them to do differently

PERSISTENT LATECOMER?

SIGNS

How do you manage a person who is often absent at the start of the day? Someone who:

- Creeps in after the official starting time and hopes not to be noticed

- Always makes excuses when confronted (often with a twinkle in the eye)

- Promises to improve - and does so for two days before slipping back into old habits

- Arrives late for meetings and often fails to meet deadlines

- Despite coming in late, stays to make up time at the end of the day - *'I make up my hours, so what's the problem?'*

PERSISTENT LATECOMER?

POSSIBLE REASONS

Traffic and travel delays are becoming all too frequent. However, some people may have genuine reasons for being late, for example domestic arrangements for children, or looking after elderly relatives.

Other possibilities:

- Unable to get up in the mornings for a variety of reasons!

- Seems totally disorganised or disaster-prone, and lives a chaotic life

- Does not consider it a serious issue (unlike yourself) and does not make the effort

PERSISTENT LATECOMER?

PRACTICAL SUGGESTIONS

- Identify the problem you are having personally with the lateness; is it:
  - The fact that the person arrives late?
  - That others have to cover up/make excuses?
  - The disruption caused by the late arrival?
  - That your authority as manager is being undermined?

- Work out a strategy for dealing with the person
  - you could do nothing, **as** it may not be serious, merely irritating, **but**
    - ▲ others may notice and pass comment
    - ▲ standards may fall
    - ▲ punctual people may feel resentful
    - ▲ absence at key times causes problems
  - keep a diary and get the **facts**; is there a trend emerging?
  - if it's irritating, caution the person but point out that you may be forced to take action if things don't improve
  - if it's serious, then take advice - there may be procedures within your organisation that you should/could follow

(33)

DEALING WITH PEOPLE

PERSISTENT LATECOMER?

PRACTICAL SUGGESTIONS

- Confront the individual
  - explain what has happened and feed back any observations you've made
  - ask for an explanation (NB Do this on a one-to-one basis, preferably in your office or away from the workgroup)
- Check that he is aware of any rules regarding timekeeping
- Explain:
  - what you want and why (stress the impact of poor timekeeping on others)
  - what you propose to do about the lateness and why
  - what help, if any, you can offer
  - how you will monitor the situation
- With the person who doesn't regard it as a serious issue you have to:
  - tell him how you feel (you **do** regard it as a serious issue)
  - reach some form of understanding, eg: agreeing to accept the situation, re-scheduling hours or informing him that you will not let the issue drop

BOSS DECIDES WITHOUT YOU?

SIGNS

There may be occasions when your boss makes a decision which directly affects you or your department without consulting you.

- You're not told about it, worse still you find out from others   your staff
- Not consulted; meetings happen to which you're not invited
- You hear a rumour and ignore it, it can't be true, or, you confront your boss only to be told: *'It doesn't affect you'*, *'There's nothing to worry about'*

OR

- You are consulted and asked for your views, but:
  - these are ignored
  - it's a token gesture; the plans are in place despite you

BOSS DECIDES WITHOUT YOU?
POSSIBLE REASONS

It could be that the boss:

- Is playing organisational politics:
  - it's part of something bigger happening in the organisation
  - she knows something that you don't
- Is under pressure:
  - there was not enough time to consult; possibly you weren't around
- Feels that you lack experience
- Doesn't value your opinion, ideas and experience
- Could be trying to tell you something
- Wants to show how good she is
- Is under-occupied so interferes in your domain

(The problem is that you very often have to 'sell' the decisions made by those above you to your staff - it's difficult if you're not consulted.)

BOSS DECIDES WITHOUT YOU?

PRACTICAL SUGGESTIONS

- Do nothing on the basis that:
  - it may be a one off
  - you can live with it
  - is it **really** that important?

The dangers of this approach are:
  - you could take it upon yourself to worry (this can cause you much anxiety and stress)
  - you could be perceived as being weak, either by the boss (who may have set you up), or by your staff (for not standing up to your boss)
  - it could happen again, then what would you do?

- Say something; after all, you have a choice ranging from:

Avoiding the situation ◀ **Defusing the situation** ▶ Confronting the situation

BOSS DECIDES WITHOUT YOU?

PRACTICAL SUGGESTIONS

- Confront your boss; two possible ways are:
  - Straight 'power play' (you are using your power/your boss is using hers); beware, with this approach you may not win!
  - Negotiate by being assertive; acting within your own rights at the same time respecting the needs and feelings of others.

  Examples of language to use:

  SELF-DISCLOSURE *'My situation is...'*
  'That makes me feel ...'

  DEMANDING *'I want, think, feel, need ...'*

  PERSISTING *'I appreciate your point, however I need ...'*

If you are expected to sell the decision to your staff, then:
- firstly, clear any concerns you have with your boss
- find out the reasons and thinking behind the decision
- jointly discuss potential problems and how they can be overcome
- if possible get your boss to be there with you

OPPOSING VIEWS ON STAFF?

SIGNS

Sometimes you and your boss hold conflicting opinions on the abilities
of people/staff reporting to you:

- Boss tells you so
- Looks to 'promote' others who
  you do not rate so highly
- Tends to dismiss your views
  of people
- Sees things in others that you don't
- Focuses on someone's good points,
  ignores the bad
- Looks for opportunities to prove a point
  about his chosen candidate: *'There,
  I told you so'*

(39)

OPPOSING VIEWS ON STAFF?

POSSIBLE REASONS

- Boss is a better judge of people than you
  - more experienced
  - more skilled at spotting potential

- Could be testing you:
  - to see how good your judgement is, or
  - is the argumentative type

- Different standards:
  - boss's interpretation of 'good' is different from yours

- Boss may be impressionable:
  - forms opinions (good/bad) based on one or two events, or even on first impressions

- Might know something that you don't

- You could be blinkered in your approach/views of people:
  - over-protective or always seeing the good/bad side

OPPOSING VIEWS ON STAFF?

PRACTICAL SUGGESTIONS

- Listen to your boss: - What are his reasons; based on what evidence?
- Present your case; do it positively, based on facts not emotions
- Be prepared to challenge (but do so constructively)
- If you want to present a different view listen to what he is saying - repeat it back in your own words before using a linking word such as:
  - *'however'*
  - *'on the other hand'*
  - *'nevertheless'*
  - *'alternatively'*

  before you present your view
- Keep an open mind:
  - Is there something you missed in your assessment?
  - What could you learn by listening to your boss?

CLASH OVER APPRAISAL?

SIGNS

A individual disagrees with your assessment of her at appraisal time and either:

- Tells you direct, or

- Does not say so directly but makes sure you:
  - overhear her views as you are passing by
  - hear her talking negatively about the appraisal to work colleagues
  - hear via a third party

CLASH OVER APPRAISAL?

POSSIBLE REASONS

- Personality clash
- Individual genuinely believes that she is better than your assessment
- Appraisal system is limited, ie:
  - may be one way (you appraising her)
  - a 'tick in the box' style which limits choice and discussion
- As the boss you have contributed to the situation by:
  - saving any complaints until the appraisal time
  - not confronting any situation (ie: regarding performance) earlier
  - not explaining clearly to the individual the appraisal system, its purpose and methods
  - being poorly trained (if at all) in conducting appraisals

DEALING WITH PEOPLE

CLASH OVER APPRAISAL?

PRACTICAL SUGGESTIONS

- Make sure you know your organisation's appraisal system; if in doubt ask
- Don't avoid the situation (any dissatisfaction could have a longer-term effect)
- Talk to the individual:
  - *'Exactly what do you disagree with and why?'*
  - *'What do you think it should be and why?'*
- Be clear in your own mind what you think of the individual and why; remember, if you are commenting on performance get the **facts**, be specific
- Agree on any common ground and identify the sticking points
- Work for a compromise ('win-win' situation), but offer a way out if the person is still not satisfied (eg: an appeal to a third party)

When it's all over, use it as a learning experience. How could the situation have been avoided? What would you do differently next time?

HEAVY DRINKER?

SIGNS

You are concerned about an individual who often:

- Arrives late
- Smells of drink (possibly a hangover)
- Has an unkempt physical appearance and puts on/loses weight, etc
- Is frequently absent (eg: stomach upsets)
- Is unpredictable (moody, very high/low)
- Speaks in a slurred manner
- Disappears for long periods
- In a world of his own
- May borrow money; always broke
- Is recognisably drunk at work
- Gets drunk at office parties and occasions
- Is known by others to have a problem but people are too embarrassed to say anything

(45)

DEALING WITH PEOPLE

HEAVY DRINKER?

POSSIBLE REASONS

- Individual is going through a difficult time (eg: bereavement, illness, depression, break up of a relationship)
- Lives away from home
- Easily led; in with a bad crowd

Note

If somebody has a problem it may lead, albeit temporarily, to drink. Should the problem improve or sort itself out then very often the drinking will subside. However, somebody who makes a habit of drinking too much alcohol could have a more serious problem, that of being an alcoholic.

Alcoholics don't need a reason and will always justify their drinking with more reasons and excuses than space permits us to list here!

HEAVY DRINKER?

PRACTICAL SUGGESTIONS

- Bear in mind that:
  - people may never drink at work, yet their work may suffer as a consequence of alcoholism
  - somebody who happens to drink at work is not necessarily an alcoholic
- Use counselling rather than discipline to help somebody who is dependent on alcohol
  - employees suffering from alcoholism should not be dismissed if they are willing to accept treatment
- Ask yourself the $64,000 question:
  'Is it a drink problem or alcoholism?'

HEAVY DRINKER?

PRACTICAL SUGGESTIONS

- Observe the person over a period of time:
  - if you know there is a 'life problem' deal with it via counselling and support
  - generally speaking, such a person will be only too willing to try anything to feel better and be quite happy to quit drinking
  - should this not be successful and the behaviour continues, then you could be dealing with an alcoholic

- If it's alcoholism, then try:
  - encouraging the individual to identify it
  - getting **him** to contact AA or suggesting that he contacts his own doctor with the support of a friend, colleague or family if necessary
  - bearing in mind that you will have limited or even no success in helping an alcoholic who has not recognised or admitted his problem; often he will keep reverting to the 'reasons' and carry on drinking *('After all, you would drink if you had my problems ... it's what helps me to cope')*

  Thanks to JRH

DEALING WITH PEOPLE

PERSON HAS B.O.?

SIGNS

There's something unpleasant about a person that makes you not want to spend too long in her company. You notice that:

- Individual is avoided and possibly isolated by others
- Called nicknames
- Gets a reputation; nobody wants to be left in the same room as her
- People play games; eg: sending bars of soap, pulling faces, gossiping behind her back
- Everybody knows but nobody has told the individual

You are aware of the problem but have resisted saying anything as you hope that it will go away

49

DEALING WITH PEOPLE

PERSON HAS B.O.?
POSSIBLE REASONS

- Person is lazy, doesn't bother to wash
- Doesn't change clothes
- Could be a medical problem (eg: anxiety can lead to over-active glands)
- A domestic problem; the person may have left home and is living/sleeping rough
- Person may be unaware that there's a problem

DEALING WITH PEOPLE

PERSON HAS B.O.?
PRACTICAL SUGGESTIONS

- Confront the individual by using the **SNAP** technique:

  Specify the situation: *'It's been drawn to my attention that you have a problem of a personal nature regarding body odour'*

  Name your feelings: *'I am concerned that this might cause you some embarrassment'*

  Ask: *'I would ask you to pay greater attention to this aspect of personal hygiene'*

  Payoff POSITIVE: *'This will help you overcome a difficult situation'*
  NEGATIVE: *'Otherwise I fear you run the risk of being isolated by your colleagues'*

(For a fuller explanation of the **SNAP** technique see 'The Interviewer's Pocketbook' by John Townsend)

What if nothing happens? Seek advice from the Human Resources and/or Medical Departments as well as anybody who may know the individual.

EXCESSIVE PERSONAL USE OF INTERNET/E-MAIL

SIGNS
- Gets flustered when approached and changes the screen
- Your IT statistics confirm the heavy use

POSSIBLE REASONS
- Can't break the habit of what they do outside work
- Does not see it as a problem or realise the effect it's having on work or on others

PRACTICAL SUGGESTIONS
- Statistics are powerful in confronting the issue
- Monitor use and if it does not reduce, seek advice from HR

DEVELOPING ABILITIES

DEVELOPING ABILITIES

WHY IT'S IMPORTANT

The need to train and develop people is key to ensuring success in today's competitive market. Consider that:

- People are a valuable resource - second only to customers
- All the profits of the organisation are generated by the efforts of people
- Everybody has ability; most people are simply looking for a chance to use it
- Business and personal needs are constantly changing - training is a way of ensuring that you have the skills and abilities to remain competitive
- Your reputation as an employer will be enhanced, as will your ability to attract staff
- Despite the costs it could well be cheaper in the long run

Remember
When planning for a year - sow corn
When planning for a decade - plant trees
When planning for a lifetime - train and educate people

DIFFICULTY SETTLING IN?

SIGNS

You take on staff who, each in their own way, have problems settling in and may be showing signs of stress. For example:

- **16-year-old school leaver** who rarely says a word, blushes easily and doesn't know what to call people

- **20-year-old with work experience**, who was bright at the interview but gives the impression of not enjoying the job, of being bored and moody, and is not showing the promise that you had hoped

- **Experienced person**, who has been doing a **similar job** in another organisation, who is not coping with the workload, is always comparing your organisation with his previous one, and is being seen as a 'know-all' by others

- **Individual returning to work** after a period of absence who appears to be struggling with the technology and systems, and having difficulty relating to a younger supervisor/work colleagues

DEVELOPING ABILITIES

DIFFICULTY SETTLING IN?

POSSIBLE REASONS

School leaver
- It's a whole new experience, working longer hours
- Has new skills to learn
- Is coming into contact with different (often older) people

20-year-old:
- Could be having problems learning a new job
- Has less experience than you assumed
- Is working to different routines, standards, style of management

Person doing a similar job:
- Could be having difficulty fitting in; possibly at a higher/lower level
- May have spent a long time (whole career?) in last company and is having problems adjusting to the change

Returner:
- Having to adjust to a different routine (time is now dictated by others)
- The impact of technology

DIFFICULTY SETTLING IN?

PRACTICAL SUGGESTIONS

School leaver:
- Don't assume he is confident, it could be a front, so:
  - ensure a proper induction
  - put him with someone of his own age group
  - give feedback and praise at an early stage
  - keep in touch, ask for his views

20-year-old:
- Recognise potential problems of coming from a different business
  - provide help during the early stages
  - don't assume that because she has been working before she will find it easy to fit in
- Ask her to give you a weekly report on:
  - what she has been doing
  - how she has been getting on, anything she's found difficult
  - any possible ways that things could be done differently (don't forget the benefit of a fresh pair of eyes)

DIFFICULTY SETTLING IN?

PRACTICAL SUGGESTIONS

Person doing a similar job:
- Find out exactly what he did in his last job
- Identify any differences in systems/procedures (can you learn from previous methods?)
- Set standards and ensure that they can be met (give help if necessary)
- Watch out for possible clashes with colleagues over job methods

Returner:
- Talk about potential difficulties at the time of the interview and ideas for overcoming them
- Possibly introduce her gradually to work (eg: build up her hours)
- Arrange a comprehensive induction programme to include, if necessary, new technology
- Make her feel wanted by asking for ideas (remember, everybody has something to offer)

DEVELOPING ABILITIES

RELUCTANCE TO GO ON COURSES?
SIGNS

Things are happening that indicate staff would benefit from training.

- Poor/low standard of performance
- Lack of motivation
- Complaints from customers and other departments
- Frequent mistakes
- Time taken to do tasks
- Requests for help and assistance
- The introduction of a new system or method

You suggest organising a training course to
help with some of these areas but
this is met with little
or no enthusiasm.

DEVELOPING ABILITIES

RELUCTANCE TO GO ON COURSES?

POSSIBLE REASONS

- People are busy: it would be difficult to get everybody together for a course

- Historical: no evidence that training has worked in the past

- 'Course fatigue': staff have been overloaded with training and are simply worn out

- Limited view of training (eg: training equals courses)

DEVELOPING ABILITIES

RELUCTANCE TO GO ON COURSES?
PRACTICAL SUGGESTIONS

- Remember that not all problems or needs can be solved by training (eg: lack of motivation may require quite different actions, see pages 21-22)
- Be aware that courses have limited success unless individuals are encouraged to use the skills and knowledge learnt in their jobs
- Recognise that there are many ways other than courses of helping people learn (each with its pros and cons), eg:

  - ▲ watching people
  - ▲ standing in
  - ▲ task forces
  - ▲ visiting other departments/companies
  - ▲ from each other
  - ▲ intranet/e-learning
  - ▲ reading

  - ▲ making mistakes
  - ▲ discussions
  - ▲ role plays
  - ▲ being thrown in at the deep end
  - ▲ manuals
  - ▲ talking to an expert

- Use learning opportunities which occur at the work place; many are quicker and more cost-effective than sending people on courses
- Make a positive commitment to look for and use such internal training - **it will not happen by itself**

RELUCTANCE TO GO ON COURSES?

PRACTICAL SUGGESTIONS

- Recognise the role you can play as a trainer at work (eg: influencing performance by setting a personal example and sharing what you know)

- Use day to day work as an opportunity to learn:
  - let go and delegate tasks to others
  - rotate the jobs that people do

- Add coaching to your list of skills:
  - this involves **helping** people find solutions to current work problems, in such a way that they **learn** whilst doing so
  - the aim is not only to help them overcome current difficulties but to help people reach their full potential
  - opportunities to coach – those who are succeeding and those who are not – occur each and every day

For more information see 'The Coaching Pocketbook'.

DEVELOPING ABILITIES

BUSINESS 1st, PEOPLE 2nd?

SIGNS

How do you deal with a situation where all the effort and energy are focused on the business and staff development rarely happens? Where ...

- All the talk is about figures and performance

- Statements such as 'People are our greatest asset' are made, but in reality little use is made of staff and their skills

- The top people proudly boast:
  - 'You don't learn from courses, you learn from experience' (This could be true but how do we know that we all learn from the same experience?)
  - 'Not been on a course for years ... I've managed to avoid them' (and it shows with few new ideas or a lack of leadership from the top)

- Requests for training are met with 'Leave it to me ...' but nothing happens

BUSINESS 1st, PEOPLE 2nd?

POSSIBLE REASONS

Such a situation could stem from:

- Business and the organisation thriving, so much so that people don't see the need for training and investing in the future

- Different attitudes of people (those at the top have made it, while those elsewhere are interested in developing their own skills and confidence)

- A belief that you learn by simply being busy (possible, but you can also learn bad habits as well as good ones)

- Bosses being unaware of how you can use people to make any business even better

BUSINESS 1st, PEOPLE 2nd?

PRACTICAL SUGGESTIONS

- Recognise that it will be difficult but not impossible

- Identify the form of resistance:
  - What arguments does your boss use and why?
  - How could you counter them?
    (see page 12 for ideas on resisting change)

- Work out a strategy for persuasion:
  - What do you want to achieve and why?
  - How will you present your case? (see page 17 for ideas)
  - When is the best time to approach your boss – are they a 'morning' or 'afternoon' person?
  - What if it's still 'no' – do you have a fallback position?

DEVELOPING ABILITIES
BUSINESS 1st, PEOPLE 2nd?
PRACTICAL SUGGESTIONS

- Prepare and make your case:
  - What training do you want and why?
  - What's the best way to meet the training need other than a course? (see page 61 for ideas)
  - What improvements can be expected? Show how the money spent will benefit:
  - ▲ you
  - ▲ your department
  - ▲ the organisation
  - ▲ your boss
- Give examples of how others may have benefited
- Gain support from:
  - others in your group
  - people who have attended similar training (from outside your organisation if necessary)
  - a credible training department

DEVELOPING ABILITIES

A SLOW LEARNER?
SIGNS

One of your staff takes a while to pick things up:

- You devote a lot of time, energy and effort to the person but there's no visible sign of improvement

- The individual is a careful worker and often methodically checks own work

- Works at one pace (snail's)

- Keeps making mistakes

- Rejects offers of assistance: *'I'm okay; I don't need any help, thanks'*

The result is that you get exasperated, and find yourself explaining things over and over again

DEVELOPING ABILITIES

A SLOW LEARNER?

POSSIBLE REASONS

- Historical: didn't like or do well at school, consequently learning may be a difficult process
- Lacks confidence, fears being shown up by others, tries too hard
- The training approach is not geared to the individual's level and style
- She has a learning block which has not been identified, either:
  - perceptual (not seeing there's a problem)
  - cultural (organisation does not support learning)
  - emotional (fear of insecurity/mistakes)
  - motivational (unwilling to take risks)
  - environmental (place/time that training takes place)
  - training not geared to individual's preferred learning style

A SLOW LEARNER?

PRACTICAL SUGGESTIONS

Work through the following:

- Identify what needs to be learnt

- Assess previous experience; what does the person know and what is she capable of? If in doubt check it out, ie: 'test' the person, ask for an explanation or demonstration of skills

- Assess the difference between the two: what is known and what can be done, as opposed to what's required - any gap will identify what needs to be learnt

- Break learning into manageable parts

- Identify barriors to learning; where might she struggle?

DEVELOPING ABILITIES

A SLOW LEARNER?

PRACTICAL SUGGESTIONS

- Draw up a learning plan:
    - What needs to be learnt and by when?
    - To what standard?
    - Potential barriers?
    - Preferred style of learning?

    Again, check this out with the individual so that she knows what to expect

- Deliver the learning; points to bear in mind include:
    - check, as you go along, her understanding of any terms/jargon used
    - encourage her to ask questions
    - allow plenty of time for practice
    - if possible, encourage learning by mistakes (what went wrong and how could this have been avoided?)
    - give any feedback in an objective way, highlighting both positive and negative aspects of performance

DEVELOPING ABILITIES

APPRAISALS NOT WORKING?

SIGNS

As part of a wider performance management system your company has a formal appraisal scheme or Personal Development Review. Unfortunately, this often meets with a cynical response. Typically:

- There's little enthusiasm from staff and often - in truth - from you!
- You overhear comments such as: *'Here we go again'*
  'Annual ritual'
  'Personnel justifying their existence'
- If forms are used, they are often filled in poorly
- People avoid the date for the meeting
- Appraisal discussion is difficult:
  - both parties feel awkward
  - comments are made that reveal cynicism, from both sides
  - on the face of it, you would rather be doing other, more productive tasks
- Very little comes from them

APPRAISALS NOT WORKING?

POSSIBLE REASONS

- Historical factors: nothing has happened in the past as a result of appraisals

- Ignorance about what the scheme is meant to do, how it helps the organisation and the individual, and where it fits into the performance management system

- Appraisal forms don't complement the performance management system

- Appraisal system is trying to do too much, ie: review previous objectives and set new ones, identify staff with potential, collect training needs on a company-wide basis

- Staff aren't trained in the system and how to conduct formal appraisals

- Concept of appraisals often raises emotive issues; for example, if the system is linked to grading people (eg: A → E, reflecting excellent to poor) or, worse still, to pay awards

APPRAISALS NOT WORKING?

PRACTICAL SUGGESTIONS

- Remember that appraisals - as a way of helping develop people's abilities - can be used to talk about current performance, agree future objectives and identify areas of help required

- Formal appraisals are an attempt to force the appraiser and appraisee to have a discussion once a year

  - however, informal appraisals take place every working day, ie: you witness somebody performing a task and form a conclusion

  - if, at the time, you are unhappy with what you see, then the individual needs to be told - don't wait till appraisal time to store up all the grievances of the past twelve months

- Don't blame any appraisal system for something that you should be doing on a regular basis; namely appraising, assessing staff; giving them feedback as well as the skills and confidence to perform

NOTES

BUILDING TEAMS

WHY IT'S IMPORTANT

Having a collection of trained individuals, you now have the potential to build a team.

Teambuilding can help:
- Achieve commitment to the task/job in hand
- Tackle problems and take advantage of opportunities
- Encourage flexibility in a changing environment
- Allow individuals to grow in skills and confidence
- Make work more enjoyable

On the downside:
- Teambuilding can be time consuming
- Individuals may lose their identity
- 'The team' could become the vehicle for criticism by others in the organisation
- Teams may not always produce better decisions than those made by experts

PEOPLE NOT INTERESTED?

SIGNS

You start trying to build your team but find a lack of interest.

- All attempts to get them to work, think and act as a team are ignored
- People continue to work as individuals, behaving in ways that conflict with everything you are trying to promote, eg:
  - not consulting their colleagues
  - not considering other people's views
  - working to a personal agenda, regardless of others
- When you get them together:
  - energy is low
  - ideas are few
  - yours is the only voice heard
  - their non-verbals say it all!

PEOPLE NOT INTERESTED?
POSSIBLE REASONS

- Maybe there is no need to form a team; the nature of the work and type of organisation may preclude or make teamwork difficult:
  - geographical divisions
  - people are used to working independently
  - wage structure encourages and rewards personal performance, so people tend to look after themselves
- There could be conflict within the group which has not been resolved
- Yet again, historical: *'We've tried that before'*
- Benefits of teambuilding/working are either poorly sold or not understood; each person has own idea/concept of a team

BUILDING TEAMS

PEOPLE NOT INTERESTED?

PRACTICAL SUGGESTIONS

Consider whether you need to be a team. There's a difference between:

A co-operative group	and	An effective team

A co-operative group	An effective team
● People work together	People trust each other
● Feelings aren't part of work	Feelings expressed openly
● Conflict is accommodated	Conflict is worked through
● Trust and openness are measured	People support each other
● Information passed on a 'need-to-know' basis	Information shared freely
● Goals/objectives are either personal or unclear	Objectives common to all

Remember, you need a team when:
- there's uncertainty about the job and the task in hand
- the task requires openness, shared ideas/feelings and trust
- there are genuine problems to face and people are prepared to have a go at tackling them

(79)

PEOPLE NOT INTERESTED?

PRACTICAL SUGGESTIONS

If you need and want to be a team, try to:

- Look for opportunities to build teamworking into your daily activities, eg: get people working together on projects, thereby sharing ideas and skills
- Learn from successful teams in sport or your own personal experience.
- Share information and involve others
- Ask for suggestions: *'How could we...?'*
- Publish your goals and objectives (is it a coincidence that the first two letters of goal spell GO?)
- Run some teambuilding activities - there's plenty of material around should you want to run your own sessions
- Keep an eye both on **what** you are doing and **how**. Could you make any changes?
- Encourage harmony and enjoyment

LEADERSHIP STYLE RESENTED?

SIGNS

There are a variety of ways in which you can lead a team. It could be that not everybody is happy with the style that you display:

- Staff tell you:
  - directly and to your face
  - indirectly (switch off when you approach them)
- You are compared with others ... Hitler
- You get a nickname and a reputation
- It gets personal
- Teambuilding becomes difficult
- You get frustrated at staff reactions and your inability to make things happen

LEADERSHIP STYLE RESENTED?
POSSIBLE REASONS

- Perhaps you got it wrong
  - came in heavy or clumsy when there was no need
  - panicked/over-reacted to situations
  - were insensitive
  - the group set you up

- Perhaps it is the group
  - not used to your style; last leader was different
  - it's a reaction to change
  - strong personalities within the group who would resent anybody!

- It could be that you've used the wrong style at the wrong time (see page 83)

LEADERSHIP STYLE RESENTED?

PRACTICAL SUGGESTIONS

- Acknowledge that there's a problem, ie: if your leadership style is causing difficulty, something has to change. Remember, **things don't change, we change**. Should you adopt the attitude of 'take it or leave it' (and there are a lot of people who do) then don't be surprised if the number of takers is small.

- Remember that leadership is about influencing people's behaviour to achieve goals. A good leader is able to select a style to suit the circumstances. No matter how many styles you adopt from:
  - directing and telling people (which has limited impact after a period of time)
  - consulting (involving others in decision-making)
  - collaborating (jointly agreeing what needs to be done)
  - delegating (handing over jobs and authority)

  they are of little use if you fail to inspire people and lead by personal example.

LEADERSHIP STYLE RESENTED?

PRACTICAL SUGGESTIONS

- Inspire people with the will to win and be better than the opposition/competition by:
  - sharing what inspires you with others
  - being visible; getting about and not hiding in your office
  - communicating your vision with passion and enthusiasm
  - selling benefits and possibilities not problems
  - being true to your word and delivering on commitments
  - staying in touch with and listening to customers, staff and colleagues

- Lead by personal example and from the front, as you'll be judged by what you do, not by what you say:
  - get people involved; without this you'll get no commitment
  - be open-minded, encouraging and showing confidence in any new ideas and suggestions (more *what if's* ... fewer *yes but's*)
  - demonstrate energy; if you don't how can you expect it from them
  - be true to your people - **never** run them down in front of others; look to support and promote them in public

INDIVIDUAL IS ISOLATED?

SIGNS

Despite efforts to get people working together you notice that one person is being left out.
Typically that individual:

- Doesn't join in
- Sits alone at break and meal times
- Appears to have few friends
- Makes little contribution to meetings or discussions
- Is picked on by the group, who set him up, or snigger when his name is mentioned

INDIVIDUAL IS ISOLATED?

POSSIBLE REASONS

- That's how the individual wants it to be
- Shyness; mixing is difficult
- Individual dislikes work colleagues; suffers them but does not share their interests, values and ideas
- Historical: one person in the group holds a vendetta against the individual for whatever reason
- Individual may have a problem of a personal nature, eg: B.O.
- Individual is not very good at his job and colleagues resent this

INDIVIDUAL IS ISOLATED?

PRACTICAL SUGGESTIONS

- Watch exactly what happens and how often
  - Does it matter? It could if it's making teambuilding difficult or getting personal and vindictive.

- Talk to the individual, eg: *'I've noticed that you don't appear to mix with the others. Is anything wrong? Why is this?*
  Follow up with further probing questions to seek specific information.

- Find out why he is behaving this way, ie: Is it a feeling that he has very little to give?

- Consider the implications of his behaviour on the team. Remember, you can't force a person to join in. However, if his behaviour is causing problems the very least you'll have to do is confront him about it.

INDIVIDUAL IS ISOLATED?

PRACTICAL SUGGESTIONS

- Give him an opportunity to succeed (especially if you believe that he has something to offer) by:
  - providing him with a chance to contribute, ie: bring him into meetings, ask for ideas
  - setting up teams which deliberately involve him in sharing his knowledge, skills and experiences with others
  - getting him to head up a project, task or exercise
  - giving him feedback and encouragement

- Running a teambuilding event that brings out the issue of participation, involvement and commitment; then turn it back to your own team, ie: *'How would we measure ourselves...?*

LEADERSHIP CHALLENGED?

SIGNS

For no apparent reason one of your group fancies herself as the leader.

- You become aware that an individual:
  - is acting as if she is in charge, eg: giving orders, making decisions
  - challenges you, both one to one and at meetings
  - enlists support against you from the work group, or even other managers

or

- You are not aware of it and fail to read any of the above signs

LEADERSHIP CHALLENGED?

POSSIBLE REASONS

- Individual believes herself to be better than you
- Jealousy: you have the job that she wanted
- Is doing it to test you
- Insecurity
- As a way of drawing attention to herself
- Put up to it by somebody else for whatever reason

LEADERSHIP CHALLENGED?

PRACTICAL SUGGESTIONS

- Remember that as a leader there are times when it's OK to let go and let others take over; however if you're being challenged this isn't the best time!

- Confront the person head on by re-asserting your role as leader (use this when you want to put a quick end to the situation)

- Develop your own skills of persuasion:
  - try to get the individual on your side, working with and not against you
  - be more assertive and firmer

- Do nothing because you are confident of your skills and position, besides:
  - it may be a passing phase
  - it may not be worth the energy
  - if you give them enough rope they will probably hang themselves

TEAM WORKS TOGETHER APART

SIGNS
- Team members are based in different locations/countries or continents
- They rarely meet: most communication is by e-mail, conference call or video link

POSSIBLE REASONS
- Advances in technology and globalisation of businesses have led to new ways of virtual working
- There is a need to use the best brains and resources, irrespective of where individuals are based or who they work for

PRACTICAL SUGGESTIONS
- Recognise that what you know about face-to-face teams will not transfer to people based in different locations/time zones
- Read the 'Virtual Teams Pocketbook' and learn about this new and exciting way of working

ACHIEVING RESULTS

ACHIEVING RESULTS

WHY IT'S IMPORTANT

Your effectiveness as a manager is often judged on the results that you achieve with the resources under your control. As such, remember that:

- You can't do everything yourself; sooner or later you will have to let go and start to trust people

- As a manager, the abilities/results of your staff reflect how well you have trained, developed and managed them

- Planning the work of your section and its people is a key skill

- Plans are ways of turning aims and objectives into actions; remember, they need not be set in concrete - you can always alter them if situations change

PLANS ALWAYS GO WRONG?

SIGNS

You make plans which never seem to work:

- What you think/want/hope/expect to happen, often/rarely/never does

- Despite giving yourself plenty of time, you always seem to be rushing around at the end

- You are always talking about what might have been and what you were hoping for

- It's beginning to affect staff:
  - they distrust you (your plans are a joke)
  - there's low morale
  - productivity and quality decline
  - people go absent

95

PLANS ALWAYS GO WRONG?

POSSIBLE REASONS

- Poor planning, eg:
  - you set unrealistic/over-optimistic targets
  - you or your staff are inexperienced at doing the job
- Unforeseen events, beyond your control
- Pressure of work
- Conflicting priorities
- Failure to consult those who might be affected
- Poor or non-existent communication; perhaps you are making too many assumptions
- Bad luck?

PLANS ALWAYS GO WRONG?

PRACTICAL SUGGESTIONS

- Recognise that you **must** have some planning skills, so.
  - Think of something you have organised successfully (eg: an event, a holiday)
    What did you set out to do? What made it a success?

- Then consider something that did not go well:
  - Again, what did you try to do? What happened and why?

- From the two, what do you conclude makes a good plan? It could be that:
    it was well thought out
  - you identified everything you had to do
  - you anticipated what could go wrong and made contingencies
  - it was realistic given the resources and timescales
  - you involved others at every stage

'If I had 9 hours
to cut down a tree, I would spend 6 hours
sharpening my axe.'
Abraham Lincoln

97

PLANS ALWAYS GO WRONG?

PRACTICAL SUGGESTIONS

- Set yourself objectives. Remember, these must be:
  S pecific
  M easureable
  A chievable
  C hallenging

- Work through the following:
  - What **exactly** have you got to do?
  - What resources will you need?
  - How will you get others involved and committed?
  - What are the critical areas? What could go wrong and what would you do?
  - Put the plan into action:
  ▲ monitor every stage
  ▲ if things are slipping take action sooner rather than later

STAFF PRODUCE WORK LATE?

SIGNS

The people you are relying on to help you never quite come up with the goods when they are needed. For example:

- People always make promises and fail
- Deadlines are missed and excuses made
- They refuse offers of help
- Panics/crises occur
- You get to the stage where you can't rely on anybody with any confidence
- There's a 'knock-on' effect; late work holds others up, who in turn complain to you, etc

> *'It's a funny thing about life;*
> *if you refuse to accept anything but the best, you very often get it.'*
> **Somerset Maugham**

STAFF PRODUCE WORK LATE?

POSSIBLE REASONS

- Nowadays, we expect people to produce more with fewer resources
- They have poor personal organisation skills:
  - can't plan or prioritise
  - unable to think or operate in a disciplined manner
- Job is too much for them:
  - over promoted or out of their depth and don't want to admit it
  - poor or inadequate training for the job
  - deadlines are too tight (or often extended so lose impact)
  - lack of resources
- Bad management on your part:
  - you delegated but possibly failed to monitor progress
  - you allowed situations to develop without taking action sooner
  - inappropriate delegation (too big a task, too inexperienced a person, etc)

STAFF PRODUCE WORK LATE?

PRACTICAL SUGGESTIONS

- Don't blame the individual(s); look at yourself; remember, staff are a reflection of you; you are responsible for their (in)actions

- Get the facts: is it the first time it has happened or is it a regular occurrence?

- Watch how they work: can you spot anything that they could do better or differently?

- Talk to them:
  - face them with the facts
  - share your observations
  - ask for their views/explanations
  - consider what you can **both** do to make sure that it does not happen again
  (see advice on giving feedback, page 21)

STAFF PRODUCE WORK LATE?

PRACTICAL SUGGESTIONS

- Help them get organised by:
  - working with them,
  - sharing your experience
  - involving others if necessary

- If you delegate jobs, ask yourself:
  - What do they need to **know**?
  - What **skills** are needed?
  - Have they got the right **attitude**? (Remember, changing a person's attitude involves getting them to think and behave differently.)
  - Can they perform to the standard you want; if not, what can you do to help?

- Make a training plan and monitor it carefully

- Ensure that key activities are carried out and essential dates are met

UNEVEN WORKLOAD?

SIGNS

The workload of your section is **either**:

- Very busy:
  - there is a lot of activity
  - everybody working long hours
  - rushing around (high energy)
  - 'time flies'
  - there are not enough hours in the day

or

- Very quiet:
  - time drags
  - people clock-watch
  - there's low energy and a lot of yawning
  - staff hunt around for jobs

UNEVEN WORKLOAD?

POSSIBLE REASONS

- It's the nature of the business/job:
  - key times, such as Christmas, end of financial year or budget time

- Work flow is out of your control:
  - demand for your products is cyclical
  - it relies on sales people winning orders in a tough market

- Poor planning and work scheduling

The result of all this is that you could be facing a difficult situation. If you have long quiet periods, then picking up again may take some time. How do you keep your people busy and motivated during quiet times?

UNEVEN WORKLOAD?

PRACTICAL SUGGESTIONS

- Find out what causes it:
  - Does it always happen?
  - Can you influence the work flow by explaining to others the implications of what's happening?

- Consider whether you need staff all the time:
  - Can you retain a 'core' of people and bring in staff at busy/peak times?

- Make good use of slack times:
  - use it for training
  - do jobs that you were meant to do but were previously too busy to undertake
  - review your work methods
  - take on additional work from elsewhere
  - reduce the working hours when you are less busy

USEFUL READING

You will find the following titles from the Pocketbook Series helpful: Appraisals, Challengers, Coaching, Empowerment, Interviewer's, Learner's, Managing Change, Managing Your Appraisal, Manager's, Developing People, Stress, Teamworking, Telephone Skills, Time Management, Trainer's.

Kogan Page have a range of practical books covering many aspects of management, in particular: 'Managing Difficult Staff', an excellent book by Helga Drummond, outlines the legal position and offers case studies together with suggestions to follow.

BBC Books publish masses of information for managers, much of which links with television/radio series that are running at the time.

'Inside Organisations' by **Charles Handy** offers 21 ideas for managers in his own inimitable, stimulating and readable style.

CIPD (Chartered Institute of Personnel and Development) produce many books on a range of people related topics.

Anything by **Peter Honey** is always worth a look. Try 'People Problems and How to Manage Them' as well as 'Improving Your People Skills'.